CHINESE MYTHOLOGY

SANDRA GIDDENS AND OWEN GIDDENS

rosen
central™

The Rosen Publishing Group, Inc., New York

Thanks to Nick and Daria and of course our children, Justine and Kyle

Published in 2006 by The Rosen Publishing Group, Inc.
29 East 21st Street, New York, NY 10010

First Edition

Library of Congress Cataloging-in-Publication Data

Giddens, Sandra.
Chinese mythology/Sandra Giddens and Owen Giddens.
    p. cm.—(Mythology around the world)
ISBN 1-4042-0769-4 (library binding)
1. Mythology, Chinese. I. Giddens, Owen.
II. Title. III. Series.

BL1825.G72 2005
299.5'1113—dc22

                                                              2005014595

Manufactured in the United States of America

On the cover: The Nine Dragons Wall at Beihai Park, in Beijing, China.

CONTENTS

INTRODUCTION

Huangdi, *the ancient Yellow Emperor, stood bravely at the head of his army made up of gods, bears, tigers, and leopards, all there to defend his throne. At the other end of the field was the oxen-horned Chi-You backed by his army of demons, ready to conquer Huangdi. Chi-You sneezed and a thick white fog covered the battlefield. It was impossible to see. Huangdi's army was fighting blindly, but its quick-witted minister created a compass and the surviving army soon escaped. Chi-You was not going to tolerate this, so he called in his demon forces with blackened skies, torrential winds, and rain that caused flooding.*

Now all that was left of Huangdi's army was beginning to drown. Huangdi needed help and called in his daughter Ba, who was able to dry up all the flooded waters. Then, Huangdi made a drum out of a sea monster's hide that, when hit, caused a terrible thunder that shook the mountains. From the sound, Chi-You's army of demons became paralyzed with fear. Huangdi, and his remaining men, rushed forward and claimed victory.

What you just read is a myth. A myth is a story. Mythic stories like the one above used to be told around the campfire by wise village elders. Without the Internet, the telephone, and scientific technology, people from ancient cultures looked at their surrounding world and tried to understand their own beliefs and history through such tales.

Myths are not the same as legends, folktales, and fables. Legends, though very similar to myths, are often based on an event that may have really happened or a person who may have really existed. Legends emphasize the story more than the significance of the story. Folktales are stories usually known to be fictitious. They are often told only within a limited geographical area. Fables are known to be fictitious.

Myths have many functions. One is to answer questions such as, "How was the world made?" Another is to justify an existing social system and account for traditional rites and customs. Myths are not an actual literal rendering of a culture's history, but they reflect the inner soul of the culture and try to provide answers in a world filled with mystery. Myths give a particular culture an understanding of its place in the world and

This terra-cotta armored soldier is from the tomb of Shi Huangdi, who was the king of the Chinese state of Qin from 247 to 221 BC.

the universe. The ancient Chinese, therefore, looked to myths to explain their culture.

Joseph Campbell, the world's foremost scholar of mythology, said in *An Open Life: Joseph Campbell in Conversation with Michael Toms*, "The imagery of mythology is symbolic of spiritual powers within us." What this means is that by understanding the myth, there may be an understanding of one's self. In other words, mythology is a way of looking at the world and our relationship to it.

1 THE ROLE OF THE MYTH IN CHINESE CULTURE

Historians believe that ancient Chinese mythology began around the twenty-second century BC. However, ancient Chinese myths were not recorded in a systematic way. For more than 1,000 years, all Chinese myths were passed down from generation to generation by word of mouth. As a result, only fragments of them exist today.

The problem with many myths that we have today is that they have gone through numerous renderings. Although the basics of the myths may be recognizable to the reader, the details may differ from one source to another. There are many reasons for this. For one, each generation may try to modernize the myth to fit into the society of the time. There may be elements of the myth that are difficult, or taboo, to repeat, such as sexual relations, or human sacrifices, and are, therefore, avoided or entirely omitted.

Regarding translations, Western scholars have used two very different systems

Shown here is a bronze *zun*, or wine vessel, which is sculpted as an elephant. Carved on the tip of the elephant's trunk is a crouching tiger and phoenix head, popular figures in Chinese mythology.

to translate Chinese. These are the Wade-Giles and Pinyin systems. P'an Ku, for instance, can also be read as Pan Gu (Pinyin). Even with the different translations, the important message behind the myths as a whole is that ancient people from around the world used them to give meaning to their lives, the universe, and everything surrounding them. The beauty of mythology is that it tells its own story as to how civilizations of the past understood how they came to be and how their beliefs fit into the society of the day. Yet it is important to regard myths as not being primitive. Some people have considered mythology as actually being a sophisticated means of studying the anthropology and psychology of a culture.

About China

What is now China has been inhabited since 500,000 BC. Today, it is a vast country that covers 3,705,407 square miles (9,596,960 square kilometers), which is about the size of Europe. More than 1.3 billion people live in China and make up more than one-fifth of the world's population.

China's history is as ancient as that of Greece's. China is not so much another country but another world. Partially blocked off from the rest of Eurasia by the Himalayan mountains to the south and the Siberian steppe to the north, it has grown up less influenced by other countries than the rest of the world.

Despite its isolation, China has had its fair share of invaders and conquerors, but these outside cultures were less developed and were absorbed into the Chinese culture. China did not experience a

The Himalaya mountains, shown here, have had great influence on China's mythology, as well as its political, economic, and social history. The mountain range includes the tallest mountains in the world. More than 110 of its peaks rise to at least 24,000 feet (7,315 meters). Acting as somewhat of a barrier between China and Nepal and India to the south, the Himalayas have taken partial responsibility in shaping China's history in countless ways.

significant influx of foreigners until the late nineteenth and early twentieth centuries. Unlike that of the Greeks, Chinese civilization has continued relatively uninfluenced to the present day.

More than 2,000 years ago, the ruler Ying Zheng conquered and unified a group of independent states. Their inhabitants spoke and wrote many different languages, wore different clothes, used different weight and measurement systems, and traded with different currencies. These unified states became China. This was a time period when a particular family at any one time ruled as emperors. The new king, or the First Supreme Emperor of China, tried to unite all the states to be the same. He was unable to standardize the written forms of the many languages. He was also unable to unify the widespread beliefs in different gods. As a result, China today still has many dialects, religions, and different belief systems.

As the population of China grew, many small farming communities joined together and eventually developed into villages, towns, and cities. In the cities, ruling families, which became known as dynasties, held power. The dynasties of China can be traced back to the Bronze Age with the first great dynasty being the Xia (2033–1562 BC). From this dynasty others followed including the Zhou, Qin, Han, Sui, Tang, Song, Yuan, Ming, and eventually the Qing. In 1912, the Qing dynasty ended for good when the Chinese military established the nation as a

This porcelain statuette *(top)* of a bodhisattva, a Buddhist deity, is from the Yuan dynasty. The Yuan dynasty, also known as the Mongol dynasty, lasted from 1206 to 1368 AD and was established by the ruthless ruler Genghis Khan. This Shang dynasty ritual wine vessel *(bottom)* is shaped as two conjoined owls.

republic. Today China is a Communist country. The state, rather than individual people, owns most land and property.

China's Religions

Thousands of years ago in China, people believed that the soul lived on after the body died. They worshipped their ancestors, gods, and forces of nature. Sacrificing objects, animals, and even humans was done at that time to please their gods and ancestors.

In the sixth century BC, the founders of China's two main religions, Confucianism and Daoism were born. The founders were Confucius and Laozi, respectively. These two religions developed before China had any significant contact with the rest of the world. Neither one was built around one central god, but they both incorporated the worship of various deities and traditional mythological beings.

When Buddhism became popular in China around the second century AD, many people also embraced it. These three sets of beliefs formed the major components of Chinese ideology and

Confucius, shown here in this undated illustration, is widely regarded as China's most important teacher, philosopher, and political theorist. As the founder of what later became known as Confucianism, Confucius strove to make education available to everyone.

have influenced and stimulated each other's development in China.

Confucianism

The most important religion, which dominated China for thousands of years, was Confucianism. Named after the famous teacher Confucius (551–479 BC), Confucianism was concerned mainly with human relationships. The teachings of Confucianism guided its followers to live harmoniously with one another.

Confucius committed his life to doing good and living in harmony with others. He believed that the qualities of loving and respecting each other were just as important as worshipping the gods. Confucianism is more a way of life and a philosophy than a religion. It is a belief that places great importance on developing moral character and responsibility.

Daoism

A central quest within Daoist practices is the search for immortality— literally, physical immortality. Followers of Daoism also strive to leave their worries behind, focus on balance in their lives, and reach peace through understanding.

Like Confucianism, Daoism is not just a religion, but a whole way of living. Daoists believe in two opposite and equal universal forces: yin and yang. Yin (feminine) and yang (masculine) underlie everything in the universe. Yin represents Earth, and yang stands for heaven. Together they create a harmony in the universe, which symbolizes the balance within the individual.

This Vairocana Buddha statuette is from the Yunnan Province, which is in southwest China bordering on Indochina and Myanmar. Also called the Mahavairocana Buddha, which means "great illuminator," the Vairocana Buddha is regarded by many as the supreme Buddha.

Buddhism

Buddhism was established after Confucianism and Daoism. Buddhism began in India and spread to China in the second century AD and became one of China's three great religions.

Siddhartha Gautama, or the Buddha, who was born in India circa 556 BC, was the founder of Buddhism. He renounced his privileged lifestyle to search for a way to escape from human suffering. He discovered that through meditation, he could finally achieve enlightenment. His followers believed that people could free themselves from fear of suffering and death through meditation and by helping others.

Chinese religion was similar to that of ancient Greece, with many gods representing different aspects of nature and beliefs that attempted to explain the mysteries of the universe. These religions, combined with beliefs in hundreds of different immortals, as well as the worship of ancestors, all contribute to the present-day Chinese culture. Under the influence of different dynasties, religions, beliefs, discoveries, and teachings, Chinese mythology now offers one of the greatest pantheons in world history.

2 GODS AND DEITIES

Deities are common in myths. The ancient Egyptians had more than 2,000 and the Hindu people have 333 million. Deities can govern over water and the sun as well as over individual objects. Mythological deities were viewed as limited, flawed, and driven by emotions and ambitions, like humans. The main difference between a deity and a person is that deities had more power and more ambition.

The Jade Emperor

The supreme deity in Chinese mythology is the Jade Emperor (Yü Huang or You Di). Some claim that he was the first god to exist. Others feel he was one of three supreme deities. One of his names even means "superior emperor."

The Chinese believed their emperors descended from a dragon god and were appointed by heaven. Early in China's history, emperors took the title Sons of Heaven.

This octagonal Yuan dynasty vase features the Eight Immortals, one on each of the vase's eight faces.

The Jade Emperor lived in the most beautiful palace in the highest level of heaven. He had a long wispy beard and wore a crown topped with a flat board hung with many multicolored strings of pearls. His robes were embroidered with imperial dragons, and he sat on a large throne. He was married to the Heavenly Empress (Queen Mother of the West, or Queen Mother Wang) who was young and beautiful and was almost always accompanied by a peacock. In her garden she grew a magical peach tree that bore fruit once every 3,000 years. When the peaches ripened, she would host a banquet for the gods. The magic peaches gave the gods immortality.

The Jade Emperor was the great organizer of the heavens and made order out of chaos. He ruled over a large bureaucratic network of lesser deities (both gods and goddesses) whose responsibilities included running the day-to-day events on Earth. Some deities ruled over nature and were in charge of lakes, rivers, and mountains. Some were patrons of particular professions, and others governed happiness, mercy, good fortune, and long life.

Each minor deity had to report to his superior once a month and to the Jade Emperor once a year. If a deity's conduct was unsatisfactory, he was dismissed and replaced by another. The Jade Emperor left ordinary affairs to his lower gods and retired to enjoy an immortal life. He had little to do with humans, and they did not pray, worship, or complain to him.

This complicated structure in heaven actually imitated the real bureaucracy that existed in the Chinese emperor's imperial court.

You Di, also known as the Jade Emperor, is shown here in this 1915 rendition. Though the Jade Emperor had many variations of his name, the name You Di literally means "Jade August One." He was the most revered of the Daoist Chinese deities.

By the third century BC, a ruling system based around the emperor and his officials was established. The emperor and his officials were the ones who made important governing decisions. There were also local officials who governed the provincial areas following the emperor's orders.

As long as the emperor ruled justly, good things would happen to the Chinese people. But when crops failed and natural disasters occurred, emperors could be disposed of. If the emperor failed in his duties, he would lose the mandate of heaven and would be replaced by another nobleman who would begin a new dynasty.

The Eight Immortals

People could relate to deities because they were once mortal and had problems and struggles that the ordinary person might encounter. When a deity had endured or experienced something that a person was experiencing, that person knew the deity understood the struggle. The pain was more bearable because it had meaning, or it was seen as suffering for a larger cause. When myths tell about the activities and attitudes of deities, the moral is usually for the audience members to alter their own behaviors and standards.

Chinese society also sees the rewards and consequences of the deities' decisions. Most Chinese gods or deities were not divine in origin, but were literally men and women who had been deified after their deaths. Such deities were part of a group called the Eight Immortals.

The Eight Immortals, who were of the Daoist tradition were ordinary mortals who, through good works and lives, were rewarded by the Heavenly Empress who gave them the peaches of everlasting life to eat. It is not clear why these eight are seen together as a group. It is possible that they represent a cross section of the population, from rich to poor, old man to youth, male and female, or indeterminate gender.

The Eight Immortals became popular in the thirteenth or fourteenth century and have been seen in many works of art. There are many descriptions of the Eight Immortals. The following represent a combination from many sources.

Zhongli Quan

Zhongli Quan was a smiling, joyful, old man with a careless air. He was rewarded with immortality for his frugal life in the mountains. His emblem is a

Shown here is an ivory statuette of Zhongli Quan. He is often shown, as depicted here, as a potbellied and bearded old man. He is also occasionally shown as a member of the military with a great knowledge of alchemy, an ancient science with the goal of turning base metals into gold and indefinitely prolonging life.

Lan Caihe, shown here, was often depicted with a flower basket and carrying a flute. In line with his androgynous, male and female, character, Chinese theater often depicts him wearing female clothing but speaking in a male voice. His claim to an endless life is that he was carried away by a stork, a symbol of immortality in Chinese mythology.

fan of feathers, or the peach of immortality. He is representative of military personnel.

Li Tieguai of the Iron Crutch

Li Tieguai of the Iron Crutch was a beggar and a healer who could revive the dead with his medicines. His emblems are an iron crutch and a gourd of life preserving medicine, and are usually depicted on the fronts of pharmacies, as he represents the ill.

Lan Caihe

Lan Caihe was a young flute player (sometimes referred to as male and other times as female) who dressed in rags with one foot shod and the other bare. Lan Caihe's soul-searching songs caused a stork to snatch the musician away to heaven. His emblem is the flower or fruit basket, and he represents the poor.

Lü Dongbin

A hero of early Chinese literature, Lü Dongbin punished the wicked and rewarded the good (like Robin Hood) and could kill dragons

Lü Dongbin is shown here. One of the stories related to Lü Dongbin is that he transformed an old woman's well water into wine as a reward for her honesty. Another legend recounts his attempts to reform a girl named White Peony from her directionless life.

with a magic sword. He was born in AD 755 and died in 805. He was a skillful fencer, and his sword could make him invisible. His emblem is the sword and he represents scholars.

Zhang Guo

Zhang Guo was an aged deity who could work magic. He was known for his donkey that could travel great distances extremely fast and fold up like a piece of paper. He lived in the seventh and eighth centuries AD. His magical gifts are believed to bring fertility to young couples. His emblem is a paper horse, and he represents the old.

Han Xiangzi

Han Xiangzi was a scholar who chose to study magic rather than prepare for the civil service. It was also said that he was taken to the top of the Immortalizing Peach Tree and dropped off, attaining immortality as he descended. His emblem is a flute, and he represents the cultured classes.

Cao Guojiu

Cao Guojiu tried to reform his corrupt brother, an emperor, by reminding him that the laws of heaven are inescapable. His emblem is the court writing tablet, and he represents the nobility.

He Xiangu

The immortal maiden, He Xiangu, appears only to men of great virtue. She was a Cantonese girl who dreamed she could become

Cao Guojiu, shown here, has several legends attributed to him, all of which express his exemplary character. He is best known for attempting to reform his brother from corruption. However, another legend recounts how Cao Guojiu was once in conflict with the law and went to prison, but changed his ways after he was released from incarceration.

immortal by eating a powder made from mother-of-pearl. Born in AD 700 in Canton (Guangdong), her emblem is a lotus and she represents unmarried girls.

The Myth of the Eight Immortals

The Eight Immortals were close friends who traveled and had many adventures together. One time, the Heavenly Empress

threw her party (which she threw once every 3,000 years) and after the party, the Eight Immortals decided they could not ride home on the clouds as they usually did. This one time they crossed the seas instead. They all floated safely on the waters on magic rafts.

One of the immortals by the name of Lan Caihe was playing a magic flute as she floated on her raft. The son of the Dragon King, who lived under the sea, sucked Lan Caihe under the water to steal her flute. The other seven Immortals demanded the release of Lan Caihe. Otherwise they were going to destroy the palace of the Dragon King.

The son refused and the great battle began. The Immortals lit huge fires and the flames and heat burned the seas dry. The Immortals rescued Lan Caihe but she wanted to find her flute.

Time was running out as the Dragon King's warriors were quickly pouring back

The Eight Immortals, four of whom are shown here, earned their immortality for various good deeds they did in life. The immortals are often pictured alone or in smaller groups, as they are shown here while reclining under a pine tree and drinking wine.

water to replenish the sea basin. The Immortals made it to land and used all their strength and anger to topple an enormous mountain into the sea so it would not be able to hold any more water.

The battle was not over yet. Eventually, the son of the Dragon King was killed and the magic flute was found. The Jade Emperor sent his Heavenly Guards down to make peace between the Dragon King and the Eight Immortals. The fighting finally stopped.

In Chinese mythology, human beings who achieved renown in their earthly lives were transformed into gods and continued their activities in heaven. Heaven was the dwelling place of most of the gods. Each god had his or her own palace, and heaven was divided into many levels.

The gods with the most seniority, such as the Jade Emperor, lived closer to the top. The Chinese had many different types of gods. Each of these gods was looked upon and regarded with the utmost of respect. The sun, moon, and thunder gods were gods of nature, and the Chinese people knew their very lives depended on the unpredictable elements of nature.

The gods were part of the day-to-day living of the Chinese. There was the god of literature, Wen Chang, and the god of examination, Kuixing. Wen Chang had assistants, one being Red Jacket, who even protected students who were not prepared for examinations.

There is a story about a young man who had written an essay but was not satisfied with it. The student prayed for intervention from the gods. While asleep, the student had a dream where he saw the god throwing a number of essays into a stove. When the god took them out of the stove, all the essays were completely altered.

When the student awoke, he heard that a fire had indeed occurred and had destroyed the building where all the essays were stored. He got the opportunity to rewrite the essay. The gods had protected him! Of course, one wasn't always protected by the gods. If that were the case, everyone would get A's all the time!

The Chinese had a great variety of gods that served many purposes. There were gods who took care of humankind, like the hearth god and door gods. Even today, you will see painted on the outer doors of Chinese houses two soldiers, one with a red face or black face and the other with a white face. These are the door gods. They are there to keep away evil spirits.

One very popular god that people still offer sacrifices to on his birthday is the god of wealth, Cai Shen. There are also gods peculiar to each social class and profession. Even to this day, people wear talismans, or magical charms, to fend off evil spirits. They may hang a picture of Zhong Kui, the guardian against evil spirits, to ward off diseases. Children carry silk pouches to ward off evil. Whatever the occasion in one's life, there was a god to be either thankful to or from whom to request something.

Zhong Kui, God of Healing

China was well known for practicing its ancient craft of medicine. Medicine men and surgeons were well respected. Zhong Kui was an apprentice doctor. Centuries ago he studied medicine, but the emperor at the time would not allow him to practice medicine. Zhong Kui was so upset that he committed suicide right at the entrance of the palace.

The emperor had a dream that he was being attacked by a demon and Zhong Kui drove it off. When he awoke, the emperor made Zhong Kui a god and named him the Great Spiritual Chaser of Demons in the Empire. Today, his painted image is credited with frightening away demons and ghosts.

Shen Nong, God of Agriculture and Medicine

Shen Nong (Divine Farmer) was a kind and generous god. His head appeared like an ox, and he had the body of a human. As the population increased in the world, the food sources started to become scarce. Shen Nong taught people how to work their land to get crops. As he was teaching the people, many grain seeds fell from the sky. He taught the people how to sow the seeds into plowed fields. He made the sun give enough heat and light for the crops to grow.

Shen Nong became the Holy Farmer of the God of Agriculture. He was also considered the God of Medicine. It is reported that he

Tales of the youth of Shen Nong, pictured here, recount how he spoke only three days after his birth, walked after a week, and was able to plow a field by the age of three. Regardless of whether these are true, Shen Nong established a stable agriculture in China by educating people on how to grow crops more efficiently.

had a magic red whip, which he used on herb plants. With his expertise, he could tell whether a plant was poisonous. He used herbs to cure the illnesses of the people of China. In order for Shen Nong to know what the herbs could do to the people, he ingested them himself. It was said that he was transparent and if he tasted an herb that was poisonous, he would see which part of the body was affected and then eat another herb as the antidote.

It was said that one day he was poisoned seventy times. He eventually succumbed to one poisonous herb (possibly the hundred-legged vermin plant). He was known to have sacrificed himself so humans would know how to take care of themselves medicinally. As a god, he was also known for teaching people how to farm, treat illnesses, make farming tools, create pottery, and create the calendar.

It's no surprise that the Chinese would look to a god to help them in agriculture and medicine. Agriculture was the basis of Chinese society. Farming life in China was hard. Farmers would toil in the fields from dusk until dawn. They lived very difficult lives, and a large proportion of what they earned, unfortunately, was given to their landlords and to pay their taxes. Peasants in the rural areas were worse off than those in the urban areas, and their positions did not improve much over thousands of years.

Plants were not only used as food sources but were used in medicines. Many traditional Chinese medicine recipes are thousands of years old and are still being used today. Traditional Chinese medicine is based on the belief that humans and their

environment form a balanced whole and any disturbance to that
balance can cause illness. Doctors use pressure points, massage,
herbal medicines, and breathing techniques to balance the energy
in the body. They also use acupuncture, which involves inserting
fine needles into certain parts of the body, to cure pain and disease
and to improve health. It is believed that by inserting these needles
into certain points on the body, the yin and yang, the qi, or life
force, can flow freely.

3 A CHINESE CREATION MYTH

In the ancient world, many civilizations had myths about gods, heroes, and beasts. Most, if not all, mythologies around the world included an account of the creation of the world and its people and animals. Of all myths, those of creation are probably the most ancient. It is not surprising that most civilizations have creation myths. Most cultures tried to comprehend their own origins and the origins of the world surrounding them. These creation myths were, not surprisingly, also found in China.

The most extensive creation account and one that appears in many Chinese sources is the myth involving the giant Pan Gu. This myth has survived in texts since the third century AD, and told how the world was created for humans to live in. There may be older creation myths, but this one remains one of the most popular and

This bowl from China's Qing dynasty bears a yin and yang motif.

involves the act of reducing chaos to order, a common theme in Chinese mythology.

Pan Gu and the Creation of the World

At the dawn of time, the universe was a dark chaos, a black mass of nothingness. Heaven and earth were not separated. The sun, the moon, and the galaxies were not yet existent.

Then an egg was formed within the darkness. Inside the egg the giant Pan Gu was residing. Pan Gu continued to sleep and grow safely inside the egg. After aeons, it was time for Pan Gu to escape his egg. He was gigantic and when he stretched his legs, the eggshell surrounding him cracked. The lighter parts of the egg floated upward to form the heavens above, while the heavier parts sank to form the earth with the sky (yin and yang).

When Pan Gu looked around him, he was content, but he started to worry that heaven and earth would collide, so he thought of a practical idea. He placed himself between the two with his head holding up the sky and his feet planted firmly on the earth. Pan Gu was not finished growing, so he continued to grow at a rate of ten feet (three meters) a day for 18,000 years. As he grew, the sky and the earth continued to separate even farther until they seemed secure about 30,000 miles (48,280 km) apart.

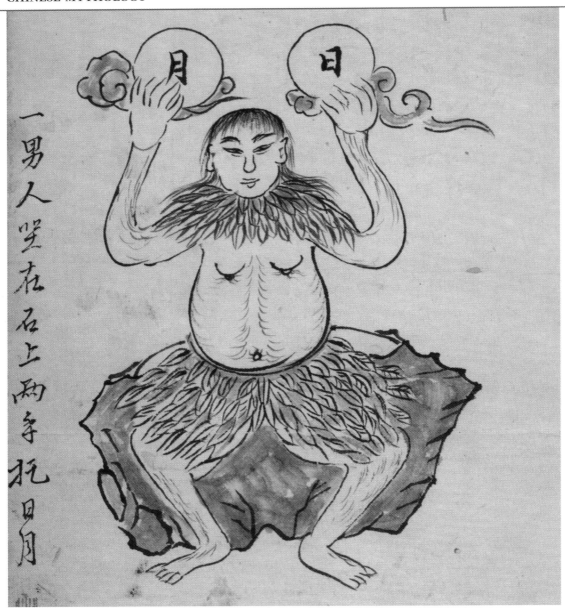

Yin and yang were integral to Pan Gu's creation of the world. The giant Pan Gu is depicted here as a dwarf clothed in leaves—a typical depiction. He is said to have had great knowledge of the duality of yin and yang. It was this knowledge that helped him create the universe, including separating heaven and Earth, dividing the seas, and placing the sun, moon, stars, and planets in their positions. Yin and yang also guided Pan Gu to create the valleys and mountains on Earth.

Pan Gu was exhausted from his ordeal. Many thousands of years had passed since Pan Gu had grown inside the egg and now he was old in both body and spirit. He went to sleep and never woke up again. When he died, his body made up the world and its elements. His breath made the wind and clouds. His voice became the thunder and lightning. His eyes became the sun and moon. His arms and legs became the north, south, east, and west of a compass, and his trunk became the mountains. His flesh became the soil, with the trees growing out of it. His blood became the rivers, and his veins were the pathways men took when traveling. His body, hair, and skin became the grass and herbs. His bones and teeth became precious stones and minerals. His sweat became the dew and the hair on his head became the stars that trail throughout heaven. Every part of Pan Gu's anatomy became a part of nature. Even the parasites on his body turned into animals and fish.

Although Pan Gu is considered dead, some still say that he has control over the weather, which fluctuates with his mood. Creation myths also have factors in common with modern scientific theory. The cracking open of the egg in the myth of Pan Gu echoes the theme of the big bang theory, which states that all matter was compressed into a single point at the beginning of time and a reaction took place that caused this to explode and expand into stars and galaxies.

Though there are many differences between various mythologies around the world, they all have certain themes in common, such as love and loss; birth and death; and, in particular, the creation of the universe. The Chinese creation myth is not much different from the creation stories of other cultures, and bears many similarities even to the scientific explanation of the beginning of everything: the big bang theory, an illustration of which is shown here.

Pan Gu and the creation of the world is similar to many creation myths worldwide in which the world is formed out of the body of a primal being. It is almost impossible for the mind to conceive of something with no beginning or no end, as in the beginning of time or the idea of infinity. Creation myths are a way for the conscious mind to attempt to explain the infinite and to make sense of the universe.

4 THE TEACHING MYTHS

Myths that are used to comprehend the incomprehensible provide a sense of security in society. Societies like to have meaningful stories to understand the hows and whys of life. Myths establish a culture's customs, rituals, laws, social structures, power hierarchies, territorial claims, arts and crafts, holidays, and other reoccurring events. They contribute to the understanding of true love and balance, self-sacrifice, and they encourage good deeds, and warn against sin, rebellion, and oppression. Myths are not only there to explain why Earth and people exist but also to teach people how they should live their lives. Myths present guidelines for living.

The Chinese culture is both reflective and introspective. It is important for the Chinese people to understand their own actions and to look beyond the surface of a situation to discover the deeper meaning. The

The camel, as this statuette from the Tang dynasty portrays, was a great mode of transportation on the Silk Road.

Chinese teaching myths include behavioral and psychological situations to educate people about value judgments and the reasons why they should follow certain paths. The following Chinese myth teaches people to look for multiple levels of meaning in any given situation.

The Foolish Old Man Removes the Mountains

A foolish old man of ninety years of age had begun to dig and try and remove the Taihang and Wangu mountains in China. He lived behind these mountains and was unhappy that they blocked his passageway. The wise old man at the River Bend came to stop him. He laughed at the foolish old man and said, "How unwise are you! At your age and with your energy, you cannot even remove one hair on the mountain, let alone so much earth and so many rocks!"

The foolish old man heaved a long sigh and responded, "You are so conceited that you are blind to reason. Even a widow and a child know better than you do. When I die, there will be my sons, who will have their sons and grandsons. Those grandsons will have their sons and grandsons, and so on to infinity. But the mountain will not grow. Why is it so impossible to level them?" The wise old man was speechless.

Moved by the determination of the foolish old man, the Heavenly God had the mountains moved, one east of Shuo and the other south of Yong. After this, there were no more mountains between Jizhou and the Han River.

Claude Lévi-Strauss, shown here in this 2005 photograph, is the founder of a school of thought called Structuralism. Though Lévi-Strauss is French, his theory of Structuralism can be applied to the mythologies of cultures vastly different than his own, including Chinese mythology.

Claude Lévi-Strauss, a French anthropologist, regards myth as a mode of communication similar to language and music. He sees that music is made up of individual parts like notes, and when combined with sound you have an orchestral piece. With myths, he sees that they are the sum of their individual parts so that each part of the myth, including symbols and rituals, reflects the whole. He sees that myths grow as they are told but the structure of the myth does not grow.

When trying to comprehend an ancient myth such as "The Foolish Old Man Removes the Mountains," you can interpret meanings on many levels. First, on the more practical level, there appears to be a need to explain why two mountains in China are located where they are. Chinese people were intrigued with how and where the mountains, rivers, and lakes were formed. Many of their myths dealt with how their physical surroundings came to be.

Second, the foolish man proved to be quite the opposite and was rewarded for his logic. Third, as a teaching myth, this story allows the culture to go beyond the surface and think that there are no obstacles that cannot be overcome. Finally, if we look at this myth in this modern age, we can understand that through natural disasters, pollution, modern machinery, and weaponry, a mountain can indeed be removed.

Myths like the following ones try to illustrate fatalism, reincarnation, and principles for day-to-day living. They tie into Chinese culture and religion in an attempt to teach people that what they do in their present life can and will affect their afterlife. Myths may reveal the fate of the person after death or the reason for a crisis or a miracle.

The Myth of the Moon

People of ancient times said that there was a bay tree and a toad on the moon. Some strange books even said that the bay tree was 5,000 feet (1,524 meters) tall, and that under it there was a man chopping at it at all times. However, the tree healed itself immediately after each cut. This man, who came from Xihe, bore the name of Wu Gang. He had done something wrong while learning to become an immortal, and as a punishment he was made to chop the life-long tree on the moon.

The First Silkworm

A father had to leave home and had to leave his daughter and horse behind. The dutiful daughter took painstaking care of the horse and one day struck up a conversation with the horse

Silk has played an important role in both Chinese culture and Chinese mythology. Shown here is a detail from a Ming dynasty vase illustrating the spinning of silk. The Ming dynasty lasted from AD 1368 to 1644. Then, just as now, silk was a major industry. Today, China produces most of the world's silk. It is no wonder that silk and silk production are integral to Chinese mythology.

and jokingly said, "If you could bring home my father, I would marry you."

After hearing this request, the horse quickly ran away and went looking for the girl's father. When finding him, the horse neighed, looking sad. The father felt that maybe something terrible might have happened to his daughter and returned home. The father did not know of his daughter's bargain with the horse. The man fed and took good care of the horse, but the horse did not want to eat. Instead, he looked longingly at the daughter.

The father wanted an explanation and the daughter finally told him the promise she made to the horse. The father was very angry and said that it was impossible for a human being and animal to wed, and in a fit of rage, took his bow and arrow and shot the horse dead. He then lay the skin out in the sun to dry.

One day, the daughter and her friends were playing outside near the hide of the horse. Suddenly, the hide jumped up from the ground, wrapped itself tightly around the girl, and disappeared with her. A few days later, the father found his daughter in a mulberry tree. She was wrapped in the horsehide and had become a silkworm spinning silk in the tree.

The Role of the Teaching Myths

The teaching myths satisfy the Chinese culture's need to understand its place in the natural world. The myth of the silkworm was very

This contemporary photograph shows Chinese women sorting and grading silk cocoons. This factory is located in the small Chinese town of Hétián, which was once part of the Silk Road.

important to Chinese culture as the production of silk was and continues to be a huge industry. The production of silk has been practiced in China for thousands of years, maybe even since before 7000 BC. The Silk Road was an ancient route that traders traveled to carry goods, including silk, from China to the West. The road stretched approximately 4,000 miles (6,438 km) from Xi'on to the Mediterranean Sea.

It is easy to see how the most important elements in Chinese society were incorporated into its most prevalent teaching myths.

The myth also reflects the animistic world view in which everything is seen as alive, including the land, even down to individual rocks. It shows that respect needs to be given to all things, as well. Animists believe that objects in nature have souls. Some souls are powerful, and some are considered weak.

5 THE DRAGON MYTHS

The dragon is the most striking beast in Chinese mythology and appears in many of the Chinese myths. The origin of Chinese dragons is unknown, but accounts of dragons predate written history. As guardian spirits, dragons belonged to the race of immortals and mixed freely with gods and goddesses who sometimes used them as mounts to ride the sky. The Chinese dragon also shows up in other aspects of Chinese life, including its arts, literature, poetry, and architecture.

The Chinese dragon, called Long, was very different from European dragons. Instead of fire, clouds came from his mouth. He had the head of a camel, the horns of a stag, the eyes of a demon, the

Shown here is a dragon-shaped jade pendant from the Qing dynasty.

The dragon is an important figure in Chinese mythology as well as Chinese culture. This contemporary photograph shows a Chinese girl performing a lion dance in front of dragon costumes at a festival celebrating Chinese New Year.

ears of a cow, the neck of a snake, the belly of a clam, the scales of a carp, the claws of an eagle, and the paws of a tiger. He could also appear in human form. Some, but not all, sources say the Chinese dragon is deaf (the Chinese word for "deaf" sounds the same as the word for dragon).

Dragons were generally classified into four types. The *tianlong*, or celestial dragons, protected the gods and palaces. The *shenlong* were the spiritual dragons who controlled the wind and rain. The *dilong*, or earth dragons, controlled the river and waterways. And the *fulong*, or underworld dragons, guarded precious metals buried in the earth.

Other Chinese dragons could make themselves extremely large or very small. They could change colors and disappear altogether. The dragon's main element was water, and it could control rainfall as well as the water in lakes and rivers. Each body of water had its own guardian dragon. The larger the expanse of water, the more powerful the dragon. The dragon was usually well meaning, although it did have fits of rage, causing havoc and creating storms and floods.

The dragon was an important and powerful symbol. Dragons were used to depict all things male, or yang. The phoenix was used to depict all things female, or yin. The Chinese dragon had four claws, but the imperial dragon had five. A dragon with five toes was the official symbol of the emperor of China. The dragon symbolized goodness, strength, and wisdom. Anyone other than the emperor using the five-claw motif was put to death.

The Chinese dragon boat races are held on the summer solstice of each year in China. This one was held on June 22, 2004, in Hangzhou, the capital city of Zhejiang Province. The boat races are held each year to reenact the rescue attempt of one of China's most celebrated poets, Qu Yuan, after he drowned himself in a tributary of the Yangtze River.

The Chinese dragon was thought to bring rain, and it is said that some of the worst floods were caused when a mortal angered a dragon. One attribute of the dragon in Chinese mythology was its ability to find pearls. Consequently, pearls are usually shown surrounded by flames, close to or coming from a dragon's mouth. For Daoists and Buddhists, it is the pearl that grants all desires and can represent wisdom and spiritual enlightenment.

The Dragon and the Phoenix

One day on an island in the river, the dragon and the phoenix found a shiny pebble and were so enchanted by its beauty that they decided to fashion it into a unique pearl. For a number of years, they stayed on the island working on their pearl, grinding and polishing it until it was a shiny perfect sphere.

This pearl was no common gem and the light it gave off was no common light. In the glow of its radiance, spring, summer, and autumn ruled together all year on the island. The trees grew so tall and the plants so lush, and the flowers and fruit were in such abundance that this enchanted island caught the eye of the Heavenly Empress. When she learned the cause of the magic, she wanted the precious pearl. She sent a servant to steal it while the dragon and

This four-toed dragon is from the badge of a nobleman from the Ming dynasty. Though dragons are everywhere in Chinese culture and art, there are minute details that set one apart from the other. For instance, the four toes on this dragon designate it to be worn only by certain classes.

phoenix were sleeping and then she hid it away. When the dragon and the phoenix awoke, they were very distraught to find their treasure gone. They looked everywhere, but to no avail.

One day, they passed the Heavenly Empress's palace and saw that it was filled with the silvery radiance that only the pearl could emit. The Heavenly Empress was holding her birthday celebration that day and brought out her newfound treasure so everyone could admire it. As soon as the guests gazed upon the pearl, the dragon and the phoenix came in and accused the Heavenly Empress of stealing their pearl. She was extremely angry and ordered her guards to throw the beasts out.

In the struggle that followed, the pearl was accidentally tossed out through the window of the heavens and began to fall toward the distant earth. The dragon and the phoenix desperately tried to catch it, but in despair could not. The pearl landed in a clear green lake. Unable to part with their treasure, the two creatures settled down beside the lake and to this very day Jade Dragon Mountain and Golden Phoenix Mountain guard the lake in the far west of China.

In traditional Chinese New Year's Day parades, dragons are believed to repel evil spirits that may spoil the new year. The mythical celebration of the Chinese dragon boat races has always been a symbol of Chinese culture and spirit. The festival takes place on the summer solstice and is thought to have once been for rainmaking, as summer rain was very important to farmers.

The dragon boat races are held on any convenient stretch of water in China. The boats are about 130 feet (40 m) long and are designed with a dragon head prow. The sterns end with a scaly tail. Depending on the boat, up to eighty rowers can power the boat. Before a dragon boat enters a race, it must be brought to life by painting the eyes of the dragon in a sacred ceremony. The actual festival originated with the following myth:

Around the fourth century BC, a minister by the name of Qu Yuan was banished by the Zhou emperor. He was honorable, wise, articulate, and well loved by the people. He did much to fight against the rampant corruption that plagued the court, thereby earning the envy and fear of the officials. Therefore, when he urged the emperor to avoid the conflict with the Qin kingdom, the officials pressured the emperor to have him removed from service.

He wandered around the countryside writing poetry, but his banishment left him in great despair. Hearing that Qin had indeed defeated Zhou, he drowned himself in the Mi Lo River. His last poem reads:

> Many a heavy sigh I have in despair,
> Grieving that I was born in such an unlucky time
> I yoked a team of jade dragons to a phoenix chariot,
> And waited for the wind to come,
> To soar up on my journey.

Today, China is one of the fastest-growing economies in the world. Though the roots of Chinese mythology still hold strong in certain areas of the country, cities such as Beijing don't have as firm of a connection to the past. Though the myths may not be as prevalent today as they once were, they still exist in this dynamic culture.

After Qu Yuan's death, he appeared to those who cared about him in a dream, telling them to give sacrifices to his spirit by throwing food wrapped in bamboo leaves into the river. He also said that the people should scare away demons and ghosts with racing boats, which had dragon-shaped prows. His friends did as he said, and even today, centuries later, dragon races are still held.

Dragons continue to be an integral part of Chinese culture as seen by the Dragon Boat Festival, buildings, artifacts, clothing, art pieces, and, of course, through their myths.

In Conclusion

While empires, languages, nations, and entire populations in the rest of the world have risen and blossomed and then disappeared without a trace, parts of China are still following many of their old traditions. Its dragons, which have been produced for more than twenty-five centuries, have virtually the same characteristics.

Today, there is little sign of the Communist Party relinquishing power in China, but the country is undergoing a huge commercial and creative change. There are large skyscrapers being constructed in cities all across the nation. Millions of people are finding jobs that earn them a spending power they have never known. The sheer pace of change is visible in every part of Chinese life, from the economy to the travel industry.

But as China continues to change, the things that remain constant are its history and its myths. Through myths, the Chinese people are able to feel connected to one another, to their ancestors, to the natural world, to society, and to other cultures.

GLOSSARY

acupuncture A procedure used in or adapted from Chinese medical practice in which specific body areas are pierced with fine needles for therapeutic purposes.

aeon A period of 1 billion years.

animistic Relating to the belief in the existence of individual spirits that inhabit natural objects and phenomena.

Ba Daughter of heaven; symbol of drought.

Buddhism An ancient religion that originated in India and spread to both Japan and China.

Communism A system of government in which the state plans and controls the economy.

Confucianism An ancient Chinese belief system founded by Confucius.

Daoism A Chinese philosophy that strives for long life and good fortune.

deity The essential nature or condition of being a god; divinity.

dynasty A family or group that maintains power for several generations.

fatalism Acceptance of the belief that all events are predetermined and inevitable.

immortality Endless life or existence.

Nu Wa In Chinese mythology, a half-serpent, half-woman goddess who created humans.

Pan Gu In Chinese mythology, a giant who created the yin (earth) and yang (heavens).

qi The vital force believed in Daoism and other Chinese thought to be inherent in all things.

reincarnation Rebirth of the soul in another body.

ritual The prescribed order of a religious ceremony.

steppe A vast, treeless plain usually found in Europe and Asia.

You Di Also known as the Jade Emperor, the ruler of the heavens and chief god.

FOR MORE INFORMATION

The British Museum
Learning and Education Department
Great Russell Street
London, England WC1B 3DG
+44 (0) 20 7323 8000
e-mail: information@thebritishmuseum.ac.uk
Web site: http://www.thebritishmuseum.ac.uk/education/asia/
    home.html

Joseph Campbell Foundation
P.O. Box 36
San Anselmo, CA 94979-0036
(800) 330-MYTH (330-6984)
Web site: http://www.jcf.org

Web Sites

Due to the changing nature of Internet links, the Rosen Publishing
Group, Inc., has developed an online list of Web sites related to the
subject of this book. This site is updated regularly. Please use this
link to access the list:

http://www.rosenlinks.com/maw/chin

FOR FURTHER READING

Ardagh, Philip. *Chinese Myth and Legends*. Chicago, IL: World Book, 2002.

Christie, Anthony. *Chinese Mythology*. London, England: Chancellor Press, 1996.

Jianing, Chen. *The World of Chinese Myths*. Beijing, China: Beijing Language and Cultural University Press, 1995.

Morford, Mark P. O., and Robert J. Lenardon. *Classical Mythology*. New York, NY: Longman, 1985.

Paludan, Ann. *Chronicle of the Chinese Emperors*. New York, NY: Thames & Hudson, 1998.

BIBLIOGRAPHY

Allen, Tony. *Land of the Dragon*, New York, NY: Time-Life
    Books, 1999.

Campbell, Joseph. *The Masks of God: Creative Mythology*. London,
    England: Penguin Books, 1968.

Campbell, Joseph. *The Masks of God: Occidental Mythology*.
    London, England: Penguin Books, 1964.

Campbell, Joseph. *The Masks of God: Oriental Mythology*. London,
    England: Penguin Books, 1962.

Christie, Anthony. *Chinese Mythology*. New York, NY: Peter Bedrick
    Books, 1987.

Fisher, Leonard Everett. *The Gods and Goddesses of Ancient China*.
    New York, NY: Holiday House, 2003.

Green, Jen. *Myths of China and Japan* (Mythic World). Orlando, FL:
    Raintree Steck-Vaughn Publishers, 2002.

Guirand, Felix, ed. *New Larousse Encyclopedia of Mythology*.
    London, England: Hamlyn, 1982.

Matthews, R. *Myths and Civilizations of the Ancient Chinese*.
    Lincolnwood, IL: NTC/Contemporary, 2000.

Sanders, Tao Tao Liu. *Dragons, Gods & Spirits from Chinese
    Mythology*. NewYork, NY: Schocken Books, 1983.

Walters, Derek. *Chinese Mythology: An Encyclopedia of Myth and
    Legend*. London, England: The Aquarian Press, 1992.

Yong-Chol, Kim. *Proverbs East and West*. Elizabeth, NJ: Hollym
    International Corp., 1991.

INDEX

About the Authors

Doctors Sandra and Owen Giddens make their home in Toronto, Canada. Sandra is a Special Education Consultant at the Toronto District School Board. Owen is a Psychological Consultant at the Toronto District School Board, as well as director of a counseling agency. They have traveled extensively studying myths from around the world.

Photo Credits

Cover © Jim Zuckerman/Corbis; pp. 5, 7 © Asian Art and Archaeology, Inc./Corbis; p. 9 © Galen Rowell/Corbis; p. 10 (bottom) © Erich Lessing/Art Resource, NY; pp. 10 (top), 32 © Réunion des Musées Nationaux/Art Resource, NY; p. 11 © Bettmann/Corbis; p. 13 © Christie's Images/Corbis; p. 15 © The Philadelphia Museum of Art/Art Resource, NY; pp. 17, 21, 24–25 © Mary Evans Picture Library; p. 19 © Victoria and Albert Museum, London/Art Resource, NY; pp. 20, 23 © The Art Archive/ Mireille Vautier; p. 29 © The Bridgeman Art Library; p. 34 © The Library of Congress, Chinese Rare Book Collection; p. 36 The Image Bank/Getty Images, Inc.; p. 38 © Werner Forman/Art Resource, NY; p. 40 © Pascal Pavani/AFP/Getty Images, Inc.; p. 42 © Giraudon/Art Resource, NY; p. 44 © Earl and Nazima Kowall/Corbis; p. 46 © HIP/Art Resource, NY; p. 47 © Getty Images, Inc.; p. 49 © China Photos/Reuters/Corbis; pp. 50–51 © Art Resource, NY; p. 54 © Macduff Everton/Corbis.

Designer: Thomas Forget; Editor: Nicholas Croce
Photo Researcher: Hillary Arnold.